T0149384

OUR GREATEST COMMANDMENT

LOVING GOD

Noreen Estes

WESTBOW
PRESS®
A DIVISION OF THOMAS NELSON
& ZONDERVAN

Scripture quotations are taken from the Holy Bible, New International
Version®, NIV®. Copyright © 1973, 1978, 1984, 2011 by Biblica, Inc.™
Used by permission of Zondervan. All rights reserved worldwide.

WestBow Press books may be ordered through booksellers or by contacting:

WestBow Press
A Division of Thomas Nelson & Zondervan
1663 Liberty Drive
Bloomington, IN 47403
www.westbowpress.com
1 (866) 928-1240

ISBN: 978-1-5127-7513-6 (sc)
ISBN: 978-1-5127-7512-9 (e)

Library of Congress Control Number: 2017901829

Print information available on the last page.

WestBow Press rev. date: 02/14/2017

This book is dedicated to my Lord and Savior, Jesus Christ. He is my inspiration for this book. I am so thankful for all his many blessings in my life and his amazing love.

INTRODUCTION

As a Christian, we can be comfortable with God's great love for us. We know he is there for us whenever we need him. We can present our needs to him in prayer whenever life gets difficult. We can think of him as a loving father in the background, as we strive to make a happy and prosperous life for ourselves. We are so thankful for his great sacrifice in sending Jesus to us and the hope of heaven someday. God is so good.

Recently this scripture was impressed upon me:

Jesus replied: "Love the Lord your God with all your heart and with all your soul and with all your mind. This is the first and greatest commandment." (Matthew 22:37–38)

This commandment is repeated many times in the Bible. This is a commandment for us to actively love God in different ways. How do we accomplish each of these specific ways of loving our God?

I invite you along to explore the different ways we can love God and to personalize this commandment in your own relationship with our awesome God.

For your reference these scriptures are included: Deuteronomy 6:5, 30:6, 30:16. Mark 12:30. They are all commandments for us to love our God.

CONTENTS

Chapter 1

LOVING GOD WITH ALL YOUR HEART

In the great scheme of life, how do we love God? Is just going to church enough? Do we have to go to church? How do you love an invisible God who may seem distant?

Our commandment to love our God with all our heart is a commandment for us to acknowledge that we are to have an authentic loving relationship with our God that is powered by a growing faith. To grow in our faith and this relationship with our

God takes a commitment of time and effort to get to know and understand him. Spending time with God then could include going to church, reading your Bible and a time alone in prayer. Prayer with God is communication. Prayer is sharing what's in your heart, expressing your concerns, thanking him for his care and enjoying his quiet presence. This is making your relationship with God personal. Close loving relationships require time, effort and frequent attention.

For a relationship to grow in love requires consideration. Jesus said," I will never leave you." To be considerate of God would be to acknowledge his presence with us and to show him respect. In living our lives, we cannot forget him. In our love for him, we have to maintain our awareness of him and desire to always honor him.

Each day is an opportunity to praise our Lord and love him. Thank you God for this day and what you have done for me. The list is endless of things we can be grateful for. It is having an attitude of gratitude for all the blessings and challenges God allows into our day. Start each day with praise and ask him to be with you for help and support, and then thank him as you start to notice the ways he *does* walk with you through the day. Those are not just coincidences!

> I praise you because I am fearfully and wonderfully made; your works are wonderful, I know that full well. (Psalm 139:14)

God is such an amazing artist. No one can compare to him. Look closely at a ladybug, then look up to a sweeping sunset, and finally look to a loved one, and praise God for all his incredible creation. God made this beautiful world, and he made man to take care of it. In respect to our God, we need to respect all of his creation, his world, all his people, and his animals, even ourselves. Try to look at everything God has made with a new appreciation, and think of any act that would harm his creation, even littering, as disrespectful to him.

In this life, we have positions or roles such as mom, dad, student, or employee. Whatever our work is, in love to him, we are to carry out our assignments to please him—by giving our best effort.

I have seen the burden God has laid on the human race. He has made everything beautiful in its time. He has also set eternity in the human heart; yet no one can fathom what

God has done from beginning to end. I know that there is nothing better for people than to be happy and to do good while they live. That each of them may eat and drink, and find satisfaction in all their toil—this is the gift of God. (Ecclesiastes 3:10–13)

Serve wholeheartedly, as if you were serving the Lord, not people, because you know that the Lord will reward each one for whatever good they do, whether they are slave or free. (Ephesians 6:7–8)

If you are experiencing difficulties in your life, talk to him about it. Ask for his help and guidance, have patience, do what is right, and trust him to give you strength. Life is hard sometimes. Praise him for being there with you. You are never alone if he is your Lord, Savior, and heavenly Father. He loves you and will help you.

> "Come to me, all you who are weary and burdened, and I will give you rest. Take my yoke upon you and learn from me, for I am gentle and humble in heart, and you will find rest for your souls. For my yoke is easy and my burden is light." (Matthew 11:28–30)

Our God is a perfect father to us. He will never leave us. He is our Creator. Every birth is a miracle from him. We can have a wonderful relationship with a Father who will always love us. We can talk to him, grow close to him, live a life that would please him, and gain eternity together in his heaven, if we choose to accept him as our Lord, Savior, and Father. He doesn't force himself on us. We have to *choose* him. That is why he gave us our free will—to choose him out of love.

> Though my father and mother forsake me, the Lord will receive me. (Psalm 27:10)

> My son, do not despise the Lord's discipline, and do not resent his rebuke, because the Lord disciplines those he loves, as a father the son he delights in. (Proverbs 3:11-12)

> "Which of you, if your son asks for bread, will give him a stone? Or if he asks for a fish, will give him a snake? If you, then, though you are evil, know how to give good gifts to your children, how much more will your father in heaven give good gifts to those who ask him!" (Matthew 7:9–11)

For I am convinced that neither death nor life, neither angels nor demons, neither the present nor the future, nor any powers, neither height nor depth, nor anything else in all creation, will be able to separate us from the love of God that is in Christ Jesus our Lord. (Romans 8:38-39)

We call Jesus our Lord. A lord is someone who has power or authority over his subjects. Is this evident in how we live our lives? In the Lord's Prayer we recite, "Your will be done." We have to get to know Jesus and deepen this relationship with him so we can know what his will for our lives is so we can give him the honor and respect he rightly deserves as our Lord.

Jesus is our Savior. The passion of what Christ

has done for us, by being tortured, beaten, and dying an agonizing death on the cross, can never be taken lightly. Because of his sacrifice, we have the opportunity to have this relationship with the God of the universe. We have the hope of a future with him in heaven where there will be no more tears or pain, only joy in his presence. He is worthy every day of our immense gratitude. We will live today for him because he died for us.

God uses deacons, pastors, and teachers to help us grow and learn. Collectively at church, we have the opportunity to worship our awesome God with all our hearts and souls in song, as we will someday with all his people and angels and all of creation in heaven. Making a commitment and being faithful in going to church or meeting with others to study is an important part of growing closer to God. To seek and find ways to get to know our God and to praise him is our most important reason for going to church and for living.

To love the Lord with all your heart is to have the realization that you are loved, that you are never alone. You are in a relationship with our Holy God. You may feel that you are living a solitary existence, but that is not true. God wants you to actively pursue his will in your life, to live joyfully and with intention, loving God with all your heart, seeking to know him, and praising him every day.

> "Anyone who loves their father or mother more than me is not worthy of me; anyone who loves his son or daughter more than me is not worthy of me. Whoever does not take

up their cross and follow me is not worthy of me." (Matthew 10:37–38)

So then just as you received Christ Jesus as Lord, continue to live your lives in him, rooted and built up in him, strengthened in the faith as you were taught, and overflowing with thankfulness. (Colossians 2:6–7)

In these scriptures we see our Lord telling us of the importance of this relationship with him, the closeness he wants with us. Our God is the one who blessed us with our families. They are gifts from him, and we carry a responsibility to love and care for them, but he is always to be first. This is his orderly way of keeping relationships healthy. Every day try to talk to him. Share what is in your heart. It might be those quiet moments in the car on the way to work, or whenever it is just you and God together.

Please know he is there waiting for you. Start with,

"Good morning, God!" Then let it flow. If you love

someone, you want to be with him or her, to talk to

him or her, to do things for him or her out of love.

You can't imagine your life without that person. Can

you think of God that way?

Chapter 2

LOVING GOD WITH ALL YOUR SOUL

Our soul is our eternal spirit—the essence of who we are as an individual.

To love God with all your soul is to have your whole being in a love relationship with God. You can have a personal awareness of his presence and his will in your life, like a close friend, where you almost know what he or she is thinking; this friend doesn't have to say a word. We could finish his or her sentences. We can have this quiet joy every day, knowing he is going to work everything out for his glory if we love him and trust him. We look at everything from God's perspective as much as we can.

> Now I know in part; then shall I know fully, even as I am fully known. (1 Corinthians 13:12)

Each day we are given the opportunity to worship him, to love him, and to be open to the work he wants us to do in sharing his gospel. As we are sensitive to the needs, desires, and feelings of the people around us, our aim in our relationship with our God is to strive for this same awareness of God. The following scriptures back up this close bond our Lord desires to have with us:

"If you love me, keep my commands. And I will ask the Father, and he will give you another advocate to help you and be with you forever- the spirit of truth. The world cannot accept him, because it neither sees him nor knows him. But you know him, for he lives with you and will be in you. I will not leave you as orphans; I will come to you. Before long, the world will not see me anymore, but you will see me. Because I live, you also will live. On that day you will realize that I am in my Father, and you are in me, and I am in you. Whoever has my commands and keeps them is the one who loves me. The one who loves me will be loved by my Father, and I too will love them and show myself to them." (John 14: 15–21)

"I am the vine; you are the branches. If you remain in me and I in you, you will bear much fruit; apart from me you can do nothing. If you do not remain in me, you are like a branch that is thrown away and withers, such branches are picked up, thrown into the fire and burned. If you remain in me and my words remain in you, ask whatever you wish, and it will be done for you." (John 15:5–7)

"As the Father has loved me, so have I loved you. Now remain in my love. If you keep my commands, you will remain in my love, just as I have kept my Father's commands and remain in his love. I have told you this so that my joy may be in you and that your joy may be complete. My command is this: Love each other as I have loved you. Greater love has no one than this: to lay down one's life for one's friends. You are my friends if you do what I command." (John 15: 9–14)

God wants to be your best friend forever. He is the ultimate soul mate. He loved you enough to die for you, and he offers to never leave you and to offer you a home in his kingdom forever. Nothing in this life is worth more than having and nurturing this relationship with God. As we try daily to find God's will for us, we grow in maturity, patience, and trust in our Savior. Through the scriptures we see we need to stay connected to him.

Chapter 3

LOVING GOD WITH ALL YOUR MIND

To love the Lord with all your mind is about us making a daily conscious choice to follow God's will. It is studying God's word regularly so we are not ignorant. A valuable scripture to go along with this view is:

> Do your best to present yourselves to God as one approved, a worker who does not need to

be ashamed and who correctly handles the word of truth. (2 Timothy 2:15)

The Bible is an incredible book of God's relationships with people. We can learn to know God by how he has related to others. It is our most valuable resource for getting to know and love our God. God has not changed. He can still talk to us. We have to have the faith, discernment, and attentiveness to listen and to seek him in prayer and study regularly.

The Bible shows the history of God, his power and his mercy, and his efforts to maintain a relationship with people. It starts in Genesis with God and Adam and Eve, then Noah and his family and many others. And then God calls Abraham and his descendants to be his chosen people. A lot of the Old Testament is a history of God's relationship with the nation of Israel, his chosen people.

The book of Exodus is God showing his great power in bringing the Israelites out of Egypt with Moses as his spokesman. God then gives them laws to live by in Leviticus, Numbers, and Deuteronomy. The history of God's relationship with the nation of Israel continues through the Old Testament in the books of Joshua through Job.

During this time the kings of Israel wrote poetry in the Psalms and their wisdom in Proverbs and Ecclesiastes, and the book Song of Songs is songs written by Solomon.

The history of the nation of Israel and God continues through the books of the many prophets from Isaiah to Malachi. These prophets were people sensitive to God and who spoke for God to help the

Israelites live in God's will. They also prophesied about the coming of Jesus, the messiah and his second coming, which we are patiently waiting for.

The New Testament tells of Jesus coming to save all who will listen and come to accept him as their Lord and Savior. This is God's ultimate plan. This is our time and our hope. Jesus is our gift from God. This is the meaning of Christmas. Jesus Christ was born, and through his death as a perfect sacrifice for the sin of the world and his resurrection, the Holy Spirit became available to us as our comforter and help to live for God. The New Testament starts with four gospels giving similar accounts but with different emphasis on the life of Jesus. After Jesus was resurrected, in the book of Acts he went back to heaven, and the Acts of the Apostles tells of the start of the Christian churches by the apostles. They spread the gospel throughout their known region. Following this is the letters to the churches, with guidelines and principles on how God's people are to live their lives as we wait for his return.

Revelation is the last book of the Bible. This book gives us a warning, a hope, and a prophecy for the future—if we are living for God.

The Holy Bible is God's truth. It is still relevant in our lives today, as it was centuries ago when it was written. There are reading plans available in some Bibles to read the Bible through in a year. There are many ways to keep scriptures in your daily life, from calendars to the Internet. Memorizing a favorite scripture can be helpful when life gets stressful. They can remind us to depend on God.

Bible studies are a great way to grow in your faith. Many churches offer studies, and they are a great, worthwhile way to connect and grow with others. It is important to make a commitment to go to a church where God's Word, the Bible, is taught and explained. The church is an organization of people—God's people—but nobody this side of heaven is perfect. Don't judge God by imperfect people, but find a church that is centered on teaching the Bible and work together to grow. People go to great lengths to find a university or college that they feel offers the best education for their careers. But our church is more important, because it is a place to learn about God, how to live for him, and how to find meaning for this life. This is bigger than a job or position ultimately.

Devotionals can be a daily blessing to start the day. They can be a new way to think of God for the day and remember he is with you. This could be a way to have time with family to share and grow in your faith together.

Journaling can be a great way to dialogue with God, to express your desires, feelings, frustrations, praise, and prayers. It is important in this communication of prayer to be specific in what you are asking. God always hears our prayers and answers them. Sometimes he answers yes, sometimes no, and sometimes wait. He knows what we need and don't need before we ask. Sometimes we don't realize when he has answered our prayers. We get so excited that our desires are realized—life can be so busy. That's why being specific can be helpful. When he answers your prayers and you realize he has answered them, thank him! He likes to be remembered.

There is a great book called *In His Steps* written many years ago about a group of people who made all their decisions for life and business by this simple question: What would Jesus do?[1] It is a true concept of how God wants us to live. It is something to consider as decisions in life come up. To know what Jesus would do, we have to understand and know him.

> Let the message of Christ dwell in you richly as you teach and admonish one another with all wisdom through psalms, hymns, and songs from the spirit, singing to God with gratitude in your hearts. And whatever you do, whether in word or deed, do it all in the name of the Lord Jesus, giving thanks to God the father through him. (Colossians 3:16–17)

---

[1] *In His Steps* by Charles Sheldon, 1984, Grand Rapids, Michigan: Zondervan Publishing Company.

As you grow in your relationship with God by studying and worshiping him, you get to realize he even knows your thoughts, and they should be in his will too. Thoughts have a way of turning into actions if you are not careful.

It is important to look at what influences your thoughts and life and make changes, if necessary, to keep your mind in God's will. If your mind is centered on Christ and you are trying to live daily by his will, it has a wonderful grounding influence in your life. All your actions are guided by God's principles and your love for him.

> The mind of sinful man is death, but the mind controlled by the spirit is life and peace. (Romans 8:6)

Our lives can be very busy. There is a constant

competition for our attention from people, the media, jobs, and our many worries. Even going to church is a very social place with many ways to get involved in God's work. That is fantastic, but it is all about him. Out of our love for him, it is great to use our talents to be involved when possible. We have to keep our love for him as our most important endeavor. God doesn't blog, tweet, or make a lot of noise to get our attention. He has already done so much for us. He just quietly waits for you to acknowledge his presence in your life and to love and thank him. It almost seems impossible to love our great God with all our heart, soul, mind, and strength, but "nothing is impossible with God" (Matthew 19:26). As we seek to know and love him, our Creator recognizes our sincere efforts, and like a loving father looking at his loved child, his heart melts. We just have to try.

In summary, this book is meant to encourage you to have a new perspective of the opportunity we have to develop a wonderful, personal relationship with our great God. The effort of building this relationship and seeking to know God will take time, but it will bless you as you grow closer to him. It is our greatest commandment!

I have included a table of the New Testament scriptures that you can use to read the New Testament through in a year. It is a way to build a habit of reading scriptures and to devote some time to God.

READ THE NEW TESTAMENT IN A YEAR

The Gospels of Jesus

Week 1. Matthew 1–6 ___

Week 2. Matthew 7–11 ___

Week 3. Matthew 12–17 ___

Week 4. Matthew 18–22 ___

Week 5. Matthew 23–28 ___

Week 6. Mark 1–4 ___

Week 7. Mark 5–8 ___

Week 8. Mark 9–12___

Week 9. Mark 13–16 ___

Week 10. Luke 1–6 ___

Week 11. Luke 7–12 ___

Week 12. Luke 13–18 ___

Week 13. Luke 19–24 ___

Week 14. John 1–5 ___

Week 15. John 6–11 ___

Week 16. John 12–16 ___

Week 17. John 17–21 ___

The book of Acts and the beginning of the Christian church

Week 18. Acts 1–6 ___

Week 19. Acts 7–11 ___

Week 20. Acts 12–17 ___

Week 21. Acts 18–23 ___

Week 22. Acts 24–28 ___

The letters to the churches

Week 23. Romans 1–4 ___

Week 24. Romans 5–8 ___

Week 25. Romans 9–12 ___

Week 26. Romans 13–16 __

Week 27. 1 Corinthians 1–4 __

Week 28. 1 Corinthians 5–8 __

Week 29. 1 Corinthians 9–12 __

Week 30. 1 Corinthians 13–16 __

Week 31. 2 Corinthians 1–5 __

Week 32. 2 Corinthians 6–9 __

Week 33. 2 Corinthians 10–13 __

Week 34. Galatians 1–6 __

Week 35. Ephesians 1–6 __

Week 36. Philippians 1–4 __

Week 37. Colossians 1–4 __

Week 38. 1 Thessalonians 1–5 __. 2 Thessalonians 1–3 __

Week 39. 1 Timothy 1–6 __

Week 40. 2 Timothy 1–4 __

Week 41. Titus 1–3 __. Philemon __

Week 42. Hebrews 1–5 __

Week 43. Hebrews 6–9 __

Week 44. Hebrews 10–13 __

Week 45. James 1–5 __

Week 46. 1 Peter 1–5 __

Week 47. 2 Peter 1–3 __

Week 48. 1 John 1–5 __. 2 John __. 3 John __.

Jude __

The future hope and prophecy

Week 49. Revelation 1–7 __

Week 50. Revelation 8–12 __

Week 51. Revelation 13–17 __

Week 52. Revelation 18–22 __

PRAYERS AND THOUGHTS TO GOD

_____

_____

_____

_____

_____

_____

_____

_____

_____

_____

REFERENCES

Charles Sheldon, (1984). *In his steps*, Grand Rapids, Michigan; Zondervan Publishing Company.

ABOUT THE AUTHOR

I have been a Christian for over 30 years. It has been an incredible time of learning about and living for God I could not have imagined the way my life has been blessed over these years by my God. I love my Lord and am so excited for each new day and the future. He is amazing!

Printed in the United States
By Bookmasters